If I knew then what I know now.

(A simple guide to helping young men cope with their reality - written through the eyes of a flawed human)

Author Jesse Stephen Lopez

Table of Contents

Introduction
- Welcome
- About the Author

Chapter One: If I Knew Then What I Know Now
- Embracing Life's Lessons
- Overcoming Challenges
- Pursuing Self-Acceptance

Chapter Two: Your Behavior Matters
- Learn How Your Impressions Matter
- Understand People See How You Act
- Crafting Skills To Help You Make Better First Impressions

Chapter Three: Impress Yourself First
- Importance of Self-Acceptance
- Setting Personal Goals
- Learning from Mistakes

Chapter Four: You Are Enough
- Take Time for You
- Help Yourself First

- Be You

Chapter Five: Slow Down and Pace Yourself

- Slow Down and Enjoy Your Life
- Pay Attention to The Little Things
- Enjoy Your Youth

Chapter Six: Think Before You Speak

- Importance of Mindful Communication
- Learning from Past Mistakes
- Cultivating Self-Control and Emotional Intelligence

Chapter Seven: Learn Tolerance

- Embracing Diversity and Acceptance
- Understanding Different Perspectives
- Building Empathy and Compassion

Chapter Eight: Better Yourself

- Personal Growth Strategies
- Cultivating Self-Love
- Embracing Life's Journey

Conclusion: Embracing Life's Journey

- Reflections on Growth and Resilience
- Importance of Self-Love and Compassion
- Moving Forward with Wisdom and Gratitude

Dedicated to Beni & Celi

Introduction

I've been really thinking lately about how I want to be remembered. Even though I have had an incredibly unique and remarkable life considering the place and background I came from, I don't think that's the legacy I want to leave behind. With all my knowledge and learned lessons, I would rather be remembered for sharing my mistakes and hard-learned lessons in hopes of educating a few people (young and old) from repeating these unfortunate and preventable challenges I brought on myself. Like you, I am an imperfect human living in a world of perfectionists. Wanting to fit in is something we all desire.

Every one of us wants to be accepted, but how often do we choose to accept and love ourselves? It took me a long time to first accept myself and accept where I came from. Sometimes I still struggle with my own personal reality and wish everything would have turned out differently. But if that were the case, I guess I wouldn't have learned all of my own life lessons.

There is no pill or pills to take that magically fixes everything. I should know; I tried a lot of them to hide from who I was and am. Drugs made me feel good in a world of pain, and I was easily addicted once I learned how to mask my pain instead of becoming educated enough to address it and heal myself at an early age. This type of education is the one thing that would have made all the difference in helping me achieve my goals and is the main thing that would have led me to success faster.

If I knew then what I know now, life would have been more enjoyable, and I personally would not have made as many mistakes that slowed me down on my own road of life. I chose to figure things out my way, which made my life extremely harder, due to the fact that I was not educated enough on society to know how the world and its people worked. I thought I knew everything as most young people do. I thought I was smarter than my parents and any other adult who questioned me.

I was a foolish rebel and was quick to fight back, whether verbally or physically. I was a danger to myself and those around me. Between my education formed by our severely broken US school system and television, I was bound to fail, but I wasn't aware of all this because I was always told I had the world in the palm of my hands, and I could do anything. Which as a US citizen is semi-true. I was born with rights that granted me certain privileges, only attainable if your family is affluent and in the right tax bracket. I was not aware of our classist-based system. As a child, I was always under the impression that my classmates and I were all equal. As a teen, it became very apparent that I wasn't going off to college like some of my friends were or going to college at all because we simply couldn't afford it.

I was about 9 years old when I realized we were a poor family, but I didn't fully understand what that meant until I became a teen and wanted the things others had. I now wish I had somebody to sit me down at that moment in my life as an impressionable teen to help teach me the lesson I want to teach you. I'm sure you heard the question, "What's the secret of life?" It's actually really simple. Life is what you make it, that's it. You can choose a simple life or a hard life; the choice is up to you.

Think about that. Life is what you make it. If you want to become rich and famous, you can take that long hard road. If you crave competition, you can work hard and become a professional athlete, or if you want to become a farmer living on a homestead, you can. The choice is yours. The trick to becoming successful is lots of hard work, and starting young also helps. Nothing in life comes easy. Most people that inherit something end up mismanaging funds and go broke because nothing in life comes easy, and they were not prepared for that kind of responsibility. Wanting to have fun when you're young is important but think to yourself about your time because your life is too precious to be wasted.

Life is short when you compare it to space and time, but in the essence of life, the human lifespan is one of the longest existences in the animal kingdom. Which means we have a lot of days to decide if we want to make good decisions or bad ones. We as humans have a lot of time to make decisions that will impact the outcome of our entire lives. These choices we make will either contribute to your own personal success or drive you in the opposite direction, possibly taking years to recover from.

I was told most of my youth that I have the world in the palm of my hands, and I'm here to tell you I was misled. I found out when it was too late, and I had already made many mistakes based on bad decisions, that I didn't have the whole world in the palm of my hands; I only had my own world in the palm of my hands. Because my decisions affected mostly me and my future, not the whole world. I thought I had power that never existed. I didn't realize I had to create my own power. By thinking I had the world in the palm of my hands, I created a sense of entitlement to a world that wasn't created for me or people like me. I thought I belonged and was a part of a whole society.

I, like many people, was oblivious to how things really worked and felt like I could do anything. Finding out that I couldn't do anything was a shocker and a letdown. Going back to when I was 9 and came to the realization that I was a poor kid stemmed from my fifth-grade class going on a 3-day mountain camping trip that we could not afford. So, I and a few other students stayed behind as the rest of our classmates made memories we didn't get to experience because of financial disparities. That day I realized none of us were equal. The next week when our classmates returned, us poor kids didn't feel the same way towards them as we had before they left. This was my first lesson in classism, and the first time I understood I couldn't actually "do anything" like we were told.

Find what you like and what makes you happy, then set yourself up for success. Do your research when thinking about your future. Stop dreaming and set goals for yourself. Be realistic with yourself and your goals. I'm a rather large man, so wanting to be a horse jockey wasn't in my future, and wanting to would have been foolish. Ask yourself important questions like "Do I meet the basic requirements?" or "Can I see myself doing this for 25 to 30 years", and "Can I live the lifestyle I want to live, working on this career path?". Answering those questions can help you decide if that is the right choice for you. There are no cheat sheets or answer guides to life. It's all trial and error. Limiting your errors is a choice you must make on your own.

We all come to a point in our lives where we feel unloved and underappreciated. The tools I want to share with you in this book are lessons I wish I knew when I was younger, that can hopefully educate you enough to learn how to love and appreciate yourself, so that you can be enough of a reason to succeed. Because you can't love anyone and build a real future for yourself without loving yourself and knowing that you are the most important person in your life.

It's essential to realize that life's challenges and obstacles are not insurmountable. Each hurdle is an opportunity for growth and learning. When faced with adversity, it's crucial to maintain a positive mindset and seek support from those who care about you. Surrounding yourself with positive influences can make a significant difference in how you navigate through life's ups and downs.

As you embark on your journey of self-discovery and personal growth, remember that mistakes are part of the learning process. Don't be too hard on yourself when things don't go as planned. Instead, use setbacks as steppingstones to propel yourself forward. Embrace resilience and perseverance as you strive to become the best version of yourself.

In the following chapters, we'll delve deeper into specific aspects of life that young men often grapple with. From relationships to career choices, from mental health to personal finance, this book aims to provide practical advice and insights to help you navigate the complexities of adulthood with confidence and resilience.

I invite you to join me on this journey of self-discovery and growth. Together, we can learn from each other's experiences and forge a path towards a brighter and more fulfilling future. Remember, you are not alone, and there is always hope and opportunity for positive change.

Thank you for embarking on this journey with me. Let's embrace the challenges ahead and turn them into opportunities for growth and success.

Best regards, Jesse S. Lopez

Hindsight is 20/20
Chapter One

We've all experienced those moments of "should have, would have, could have," replaying in our minds, wishing we had acted differently. Whether it's due to an accident or a mistake, these reflections are a part of life. As humans, we're bound to make mistakes, but it's crucial to understand the distinction between accidents and choices. Consider the analogy of moving boxes: rushing to stack them high for quick completion versus stacking them lower for better visibility, avoiding potential accidents. It's in these split-second decisions that we can find ourselves in the realm of "should have, would have, could haves."

This understanding can guide us in minimizing the mistakes we make in our daily lives. Not all errors are as straightforward as crashing boxes. At the age of 17, I made a single mistake that led to a felony conviction for possession of marijuana at 18. This mistake profoundly impacted my life, teaching me a harsh lesson about the consequences of breaking the law. I argued then that marijuana was harmless and would eventually be legalized, but I learned the hard way that life doesn't always align with our beliefs, and fairness is not guaranteed.

I had the opportunity to reform myself and clean up my act, but I chose the easier path of living day by day without taking responsibility for my future. My friends and I indulged in parties, day drinking, and reminiscing about high school while watching our peers embark on successful careers. We blamed external factors for our situations, failing to realize that our choices were shaping our outcomes.

Instead of making a plan for my future, I delved deeper into selling drugs for quick money, ignoring the potential a well-paying job or education could offer. I fell into the trap of easy money, not realizing the heavy toll it would take on my life and well-being. It's crucial to understand that shortcuts often lead to dead ends, and true success requires dedication, hard work, and perseverance.

The world of illegal activities is a risky and unstable one, filled with unreliable sources and dangerous stereotypes. The allure of fast cash comes at a significant cost, both morally and personally. Climbing the ladder of illicit success only leads to a life of constant fear, where every moment is overshadowed by the looming threats of law enforcement and rival criminals.

It's time to break free from the cycle of destructive choices and start envisioning a real future. Picture the life you want, the home you see yourself in, and the path to get there. Set realistic goals, stay focused, and believe in your ability to achieve greatness. Excellence takes time and effort, but every step forward brings you closer to your full potential.

As creators of our destinies, we hold the power to shape our futures. The past may haunt us, but it doesn't define us. By learning from our mistakes and planning for a better tomorrow, we can overcome any obstacle and build a life of purpose and fulfillment. Remember, what you do today shapes your tomorrow. Don't let regrets define your journey. Embrace the lessons, learn from the past, and forge ahead with determination and resilience.

Your Behavior Matters

Chapter Two

Most of us have heard the expression "First impressions are the most important," which is somewhat true. The reality of this statement is that every impression matters most. Your first impression is nothing more than an introduction. Every interaction after that is just as important, and to insinuate that the first is more important than every other interaction allows one to believe they must play a part, or an acting role to gain acceptance which should only be presented once in an initial meeting, and that's simply not true.

There's nothing genuine about acting like you're something you're not. This form of acting can be viewed as misleading, and as you drop the act, the people around you will feel you're untrustworthy and disingenuous as you reveal your true self. If you want people to like and accept you, be the person that people like and want to be around.

I'm guilty of both falsely presenting myself as something I wasn't in first impressions, and just showcasing bad behavior all around. I grew up in a low-income neighborhood but went to school with an evenly mixed group of upper middle-class and us poor kids. Right in my face daily, I saw and watched kids whose parents bought them fast food meals delivered by mommy or a nanny, all the way down to kids that couldn't afford lunch at all. This created shame in my own mind towards my own personal upbringing. So, the lying began. A little white lie here or there just to fit in never hurt anyone, right?

This is another moment in my life. I wish I had someone to tell me to be proud of who I was and am because the lies I told weren't only heard by those I told the lies to. I was also hearing the lies I was telling to fit in, which made me start to believe them, corrupting my own idea of who I was. Instead of being me, I was playing a part, all to fit in.

Most of the people I wanted to hang out with or like me in my youth are long gone and forgotten memories, and some of these people's memories of me are of a liar all because I wanted to fit in. Whether it was me wanting clothing brands or sneakers that I could not afford; I was becoming the character I was playing and not me. After a few years of lies, I didn't even know who I was anymore. Not being honest with who I was at this time has always been one of the biggest regrets of my life because it made me lose sight of who I really was.

It's crazy to think of the power of influence. We as humans were born with one of the most powerful brains on our planet. But that brain can easily be influenced by others, and it is mostly influenced by ourselves. Our peers and the people we want to befriend can also play a part in influencing your persona, but you are the one that can choose to be influenced or not.

As a young child, I was always into art, music, and loved to sing and dance. But as I got older those hobbies and interests faded because they weren't cool things to do. So, I stopped drawing, and singing, and started gangbanging, drinking, and doing drugs with other kids who lost their selves too. I didn't have anyone to guide me back to the path of success, so I just kept on my path to destruction. I destroyed friendships, job opportunities, a marriage, a relationship with my kids, and any chance at a respectable life I could imagine because once I didn't know who I was, I didn't know what direction I needed to go in. I was a lost cause and didn't want to be helped.

I was no longer me; I was now a thug and a drug dealer that had to play the part. Think to yourself for a quick second about how thugs and drug dealers are perceived in our society. They are viewed as rejects and criminal scum that you probably wouldn't leave your daughter around, right? Well, that's the role I was playing. Surrounded by guns, thugs (aka other broken young men), drugs, and lots of bad energy. Retaliation was a way of life. Eye for eye. This negative energy took over my soul, and I was fully corrupted.

With a pocket full of money, and a gun on my hip daily, I felt unstoppable. Knowing people feared me added to my ego and drove me to wanting more power. Power that was easily taken away by law enforcement time and time again. A power that would place me in jail several times throughout my youth and into my adult years. I brought shame to my family and even financial hardships due to my bad decisions, and I did this over and over because I was afraid of changing and learning who I really was.

What I would like for you to do is think about where you are in your life. Do you know who you really are? Or do you only know the person you've become as you've tried to fit in? What are your interests? What things do you keep secret that is something you wish others knew about you?

I'm here to tell you that you're not your social media persona; you are you. The person you are hiding from. The person that you think is dorky or strange. That's who you are. Learn who you are when you're young, and don't be like me having to figure it out late in life.

My bad behavior put me in several bad situations because I wanted to be a boss, the leader, the head honcho, and all that got me was a life of struggles and trauma that all could have easily been avoided if I had just enjoyed life and been myself. If you learn one thing from this chapter, I hope it's this: it's okay to be yourself because the real you is the most important version of yourself you can be. Don't let others pave your road of life; do it yourself. The hard work will pay off, I promise.

These days I am a graduate of Cornell University and an acclaimed published writer because after years of searching I finally found the real me. My whole life was put on hold due to my bad behavior. I didn't have a family or a mentor to help me along life's struggles or anyone to help me along the way. I hope each chapter you read helps you understand how important and powerful you are as a human being. I also hope you understand how easy it is to choose a path that leads to failure. These choices are all up to you.

Today you can choose to start to better your life and help the person you need to care about most, yourself. Or you can ignore my message to you and see where you end up. The choice is yours. From my own personal experience, I found education is something that helped me in finding my real self. I have always been a bit nerdy or geeky. I like learning new things. But being a nerdy thug just wasn't realistic. That's why it took me years to find out that my passion was writing and helping others see things through a different perspective.

We now live in a world based on two things: perception and reality. Perception is tricky. Things like marketing allow for perception to fog reality and trick someone into thinking something is something it's not. Reality is simple; it's real. Not fake or misleading, it's fact. But these two are commonly misconstrued as the same thing. Our perception of things is the way we want to see things turn out, and reality is the simple outcome of life.

No matter how good of a person you are, other people's perception of you is based on the behaviors they've seen you display. That's why your behavior matters so much. You can say as many times as you want that you don't care about what people think of you. But that's all nonsense. We all care about what others think of us; it's just human nature. Instead of playing a part, just be confident in who you are, and the real you will shine through. Life isn't easy, and how you behave plays a big part in how your life will turn out. The choice is up to you; just keep in mind that the real you is smarter and better than the character you are playing.

Impress Yourself First

Chapter Three

Nothing feels better than a pat on the back for a job well done. If you're like me, it's uplifting and can really boost endorphins, feeling satisfying. I think it's fair to say something we all dislike is when we do the opposite and let someone we care about down. That feeling of disappointment can linger and agitate our behaviors, allowing for depression or anxiety to set in. Later, I will talk more about those topics, but for now, let's focus on impressing yourself first.

Our peers, friends, and family members all influence us and help mold the people we become. On planet Earth, there is a lot going on at once, and it's easy to see how many of us humans can feel insignificant at times in our existence. But the truth is, you and I are members of the smartest and most dangerous species of animal on this planet, and each and every one of us can make a difference and change things in our reality.

If you want something, you can have it. It just takes hard work. Rockets fly to outer space as a norm. Everyone, for the most part, carries around a small computer called a smartphone in their pockets. People are constantly doing the unthinkable, and so can you. You just have to put yourself first.

I didn't put myself first and realized I needed to build up my own power. So, I sought after being accepted by anyone or any group that would show me acceptance, and I morphed to fit in. It's what we all do to passively fit in. I did what I thought I needed to do, and I adapted. I even learned how to perfectly "code-switch" my Latino characteristics away. I was too busy trying to fit in and impress the wrong people.

I didn't stop for a second and thought about my future. It wasn't important to me. My friends and my life at that time were all that mattered. I didn't take my jobs, relationships, or life seriously. It was all about impressing these people so they could keep filling the void education would have filled. And so, my path to success became farther in the distance as I forged my own path without a plan.

I come from a family where mental health disorders run deep. Asking them for help was out of the question. Seeking advice from my inner circle would have shown weakness, and in that world, weakness is the last thing you can show. I had to foot the bill and be happy about it because that was the cost of being the boss. I sold drugs to fund drug and alcohol-induced nights that normally ended in fights, car accidents, damaged property, and pretty much any dramatic situation you can think of, just to be repeated the next day. I never once impressed myself first.

When you set goals for yourself and accomplish them, it bears a sense of accomplishment that is unmatched on a personal level. It is a way for you to be proud of yourself, a form of self-communication. You tell yourself (the inner you) that you can do something. Whether it be a simple task or something far more treacherous, when you tell yourself you can do it, a small inter-competition with your will and power begins, and you slowly start to learn more about your abilities, capabilities, and your inabilities.

From as far back as I can remember, I have always had a need to crack jokes and be funny. More than likely, it stemmed from me being the youngest in my family and wanting to be heard, or maybe it was me hiding my feelings of un-comfortability as I was always the fattest kid in the room; I'm not sure. But humor became my blanket of armor, and I used it for protection. Being quick-witted was a skill I crafted and used like a weapon every time my feelings were hurt or provoked. I was different from most of the kids my age because being poor meant you had to be resourceful and figure things out on your own.

My Pops wasn't around ever, and when I was home, my mom worked a full-time job, so there wasn't much time to be taught how to do things. We all had to figure it out on our own. My mom was disowned from her Catholic family over her choice to join the Jehovah's Witness religion, so we weren't really raised around our grandparents, aunts, uncles, and cousins and didn't receive much support from them, if any at all. It was just us all fending for ourselves. What made matters worse was that the low-income neighborhood we grew up in was 25 miles away from the city of

Tucson in a small town called Catalina, Arizona, smack dab in the middle of nowhere.

We had to figure everything out on our own. Life was tough. Going through changes and not having anyone to talk to about it. Wondering if I'm a freak or were my feelings normal. Many of us poor kids found refuge in lying. It was a way to create the world we wanted to live in rather than the life we were given. Not having a family allowed for the imagination to run wild, as there were no traditions or recollections to draw from. We were a blank canvas waiting to be painted.

As the youngest in my family, I have never been taken seriously. I was always looked down upon and hated the feeling of not being respected, so I fled my family in search of friends that would replace the family I never wanted with people that took full advantage of my kindness and yearning for acceptance. My weakness was and always has been family. Family is easier to run from than face. I can't speak for those who had parents that cared about them because that is a world I lack knowledge in.

Because I was too busy impressing others, when I finally became an adult and made my own family in my early 20s, I ruined my marriage, my family, and the opportunity to raise my children. This is one of the hardest things for me to talk about and deal with. I have always regretted walking away from my kids' lives. My wisdom tells me that they were better off without me since I was in such a destructive place at that time in my life. But the hardest part of my life has been not having them in my life the way I wish I could. My bad behavior and selfish actions have left me scarred and in pain to this very moment, and I'm sure until the day I die. But this was my choice, and I was wrong.

The reason I'm writing this book is to hopefully help you not make the same mistakes I made. I was stupid for believing others' acceptance and attention was so important. We all are going to have our own demons we are going to have to face in our lifetime, but you can do the opposite of what I did and do better. The feelings of disappointment I have faced were mostly brought on by myself.

I could have woken up every day and said enough is enough and found my way back to my path to success, but I didn't. By the time I did reach out to try to rekindle my relationship with my kids, I was denied and asked to leave. That was the worst day of my lived life, but it was fully my fault because of my bad decisions. My imperfect and immoral behavior allowed me to lose my entire family.

Redemption is possible. You just must be willing to put yourself first. There will be many uncomfortable moments in your life that you can be prepared for if you start now and create your plan. As I said in the last chapter, you can't be afraid of failure. Failure is truly one of the best ways to learn, but it's not always the best version of learning.

The best thing you can learn is who you are. Not where you fit in or who you want to befriend. The best thing you can learn again is "who you are". You're not going to know where you'll be living in ten or twenty years, or what exact job you'll have either. By learning something new each day, you can feed your brain the information it needs to process if the thing you are doing is either enjoyable or boring. Learning your likes and dislikes can help you choose a career path that will be more suitable for the lifestyle you want to live.

If you're like me and enjoy nice new things, then you need to think of how you can realistically obtain these things and still maintain a healthy balance of life, love, and stress. These again are all choices you get to make each and every day. You can live paycheck to paycheck barely getting by while playing keeping up with the Joneses. Or you can work hard, get a higher-paying career, and be able to live how you want; the choice is yours.

How important are the people you are trying to impress? How much have they done to better or advance your life? Are they truly your friends, or just someone to pass the time with? What are you willing to do for them to better or advance their lives? These are questions that can start you thinking about the people you have in your life. It's okay to be friends with people who aren't like you but be realistic with yourself. Because I put my friends first, I lost years of my life that I could have enjoyed with my loved ones and children.

Regretting life sucks. I would know; I catch myself doing it all the time; it's one of my many bad habits. I'm probably halfway through my life cycle, and I barely caught on. I wish now that I did the things that made me happy. I wish that in my younger years, I had put myself first and started my life plan at an earlier time in my life like you can. I have had to write a lot of wrongs in my lifetime, and I have caused myself pain that wasn't necessary, all because I wasn't willing to put myself first and impress myself first.

Remember again that the secret to life is that life is what you make it. I made my life harder, as a lot of people have done, all because we had to figure it out on our own. These lessons many of us learned from could have been prevented if we were educated enough to know having a life plan could have saved us all a lot of time and money.

Tomorrow when you wake up, you can choose to impress yourself first or put others first by impressing them. Think about what a future is really like. Bills never stop, and life never stops happening. Life is hard; you can choose to make it easier on yourself or harder. I messed up and took the harder route; I hope you can see how wrong I was. I hope my mistakes can be a lesson to you and keep you on your road to success.

You Are Enough

Chapter Four

Humans have always loved a good heroic story where someone saves the day. The idea of that hero has morphed and evolved into our present-day superhero movies. We humans have a fascination with superpowers. The truth is we are all superheroes with superpowers. Maybe we can't stick out our arm like old Clark Kent, but we can fly on an airplane. Each and every one of our brains possesses different types of superpowers that can help change someone's life or save our planet. You just must know who you truly are before you can understand which powerful gifts you were given.

Most of my younger years were spent hiding from myself underneath a blanket of drugs and alcohol. Peeking out at the world, afraid of my future like a scared child hiding from the dark of night in their bed. To me, my future wasn't important because I had a house, cars, semi-nice things, and enough money to survive. In my eyes, I had made it selling drugs, and working my shitty part-time jobs as a line cook or chef that paid just enough to keep people from questioning my income. I thought I was fooling the system. My gift is the power of persuasion. I can convince anyone to do just about anything; it's always been the most powerful gift I was given.

For me, this helped me lie and deceive people daily. I learned how to use my power in the wrong way. Like Darth Vader, I wanted to be on the dark side. Having my friends sell drugs and commit felony crimes for me instead of supporting them in their dreams and futures made me money, so that's the way things went. I profited from their shortcomings and lack of motivation for life. I handed them an easy job that made them a good chunk of change, that ended up costing some of their freedom and a few of their lives.

I knew the whole time I could have been doing better, but I didn't. I never realized that each day I lived like this was another day lost forever from the life deep down I truly wanted to be living. My decisions ruined families, people's lives, and the community I was raised in. I kept me and the people around me blacked out enough on cocaine and benzodiazepines (Xanax) from ever seeing our future. We were like walking zombies with jewelry dressed in designer clothing with guns, paranoid by any stranger looking our way. I created an unsafe environment, all while starting a family. I had everyone living in danger, and it was all my fault.

Realizing you are enough is important for yourself and your future. It's something I fully regret not knowing until it was too late. This kind of self-wisdom can keep you grounded, realizing how important being yourself is and knowing you're enough of a reason to succeed. We hear it all the time, "my children are my reason" or "I did this all for you," and we have been conditioned to think that when you say something as bold as "I did this for me," that we aren't humble or genuine. You are enough of a reason. That's not selfish or egotistical to believe.

Life can change at any moment and the people you love today may not be around in your future. Whether due to death or due to removing these individuals from your life, things will change. Children die before their parents, marriages end, and families can be broken up; it's all just part of life. Putting "yourself" first isn't selfish; it means you are focusing on how to be the best version of you to those in your life at any given time and place. It's about educating yourself on the topic of you.

What do you like? What kinds of things make you happiest? Who are the people you admire most? What places do you want to see or travel to? Can you do things alone?

If you're like me when I was younger, then you probably like being surrounded by people all the time to distract you from achieving excellence. Distractions are you accepting mentally that your life plan can be put on hold. It okays these behaviors as your thoughts are now focused on the distraction instead of you bettering your life. Other people's drama, television, social media, and video games are all easy ways for us to hide from ourselves and the things we could be accomplishing. We slump, sigh, and moan as we watch others' lives unfold before our eyes, denying we could do similar things. We talk about how well others are doing and never appreciate our own personal struggle because we were raised in a "No Sniveling" kind of world.

It's okay to like other things from your friends and family. You are a unique individual; explore your likes and meet new people that like the things you do that are from outside your circle. We are products of our environment, but we don't have to be products stuck in that environment. Branch out, try new foods, talk to strangers in line, complement people for their work. Don't hold back because someone might think you're uncool or weird like I did. I was wrong, and I suffer dearly for it.

What I didn't understand was that if I had built a life plan and stuck to it, I could still have fun, live a good life, and better myself all at once. I had 24 hours each day to make the changes that would have helped me become a better and more successful version of me. I was too busy not realizing that I was enough of a reason. I was impressing the wrong people and hating myself for it.

It's hard to admit when you are wrong; trust me I know. It's no fun to have to look someone in the eyes and apologize for something that could have been fully avoided. I have had to look into my friends' mothers' eyes to tell them I'm sorry for their son dying from an overdose of drugs I had them selling. I've hugged a sister to a friend that died leaving one of my parties too drunk to drive, apologizing for letting them leave. I've paid bills for friends that were sent to jail or prison for doing my dirt. I have had so many regrets and a harder life that was brought on by my own stupidity and ignorance.

The power you possess can become the thing that guides you to success. You might have a hidden talent, be gifted at mathematics or science, or have the heart for helping others. But to activate these powers, you must put yourself first so that you can learn as much as you can about your strengths and powers and use them to your benefit rather than your destruction like I did. You can do anything that you're willing to work hard enough to achieve. But the trick is hard work, and you have to choose dedication and personal commitment.

Your friends, family, and loved ones are important. Having a life that allows you to raise a family and be successful can be achievable. To get there, you must put yourself first and know that you are enough of a reason to succeed.

Slow down and pace yourself

Chapter Five

Because I made fast money, I lived a fast life. Always trying to act older than I really was. I was the youngest kid in my class, and always the youngest in my group of friends. Being as I was the youngest in my family, I felt I had to prove to everyone else that I wasn't just some little kid. I was acting my part, like a role that was written for the silver screen, a real blockbuster.

Without a dad around and a mom that worked long hours, us kids had a lot of unsupervised time on our hands. We could do just about anything if it was cleaned by 6 pm when mom was back home. We were bad kids and so we did what bad kids do. We drank alcohol and smoked weed all before 5th grade. I was 11 the first time I tried cocaine, and only 10 years old the first time I ever blacked out from drinking 40 oz'ers of malt liquor. The people my sisters hung out with were older, the people I hung out with were older, so I acted older.

I lost most of my childhood to acting older and tougher than I was. I fought older kids, dated, and messed around with older girls. All this forced me to stop liking age-appropriate things like cartoons and movies, to watching porn, listening to rap, and wanting to party like an older person. Remember when you were a kid and your parents told you, "That's not for you, that's for adults"? Things like R-Rated movies, drinking alcohol, or smoking cigarettes? Yeah, those are the things we immediately gravitated to.

Drinking our parents' booze and replacing it with water. Stealing a single cigarette or two here and there from those parents that smoked. Going through all of our parents' things to see what we could find.

We learned about drugs at an early age. The older siblings and cousins of my friends and family were trying new things and experimenting with drugs. Because we had such a huge gap in the day of no one being home, you could easily ditch school, try a drug, get fucked up, and have enough time to recover and answer the recorded absence message on the phone from the school well before any adult arrived home from their day at work.

We were too cool for sports or our teammates we thought. School and classes felt like a waste of time. Hanging out with our friends was easier than taking tests or reading. We were quick to do the grown-up things like drink, smoke, and party, but we weren't grown-up. So, all we looked like was a bunch of wasted talent. Once all the failures started adding up like bad grades, losing friends over being bad influences, fighting, getting arrested, and being kicked out of school, we started resenting the world for punishing us for our bad decisions.

Things like fines and speeding tickets became how we spent our money. We lost the opportunity to be young. I see kids in public acting obnoxious and find myself thinking how annoying they are and how I would have never acted like that. Then I realize that I didn't have moments like that where I was being a carefree kid. I was too busy playing my part. Next time you hear some annoying kids think about how awesome it must be to be having that much fun to not be caring about what anyone else thinks. That's something I never experienced, and I personally think moments like that are the most beautiful moments of our lives.

So many of my regrets span from me always wanting to grow up so fast. Life is fragile, and we can easily become damaged. We are sensitive and emotional beings. Everything we do or don't do comes from your emotional drive. You either want to do something or you don't. Ever say, "I don't feel like doing that"? That's your emotions blocking your power and slowing you down on your road to success. Think about those people you admire the most I asked you about in the last chapter. What are the things that draw you to that person? Is it their talent? Their wealth? Or maybe their possessions?

Maybe you like an athlete like a basketball player. Have you ever thought about how many shots it takes to become as skilled as they are? If you're their biggest fan and have watched every single one of their games, did you ever think about how much time they spent practicing, or how many hours spent on their own time were used to perfect their craft? Some of us are lucky and are born with talents that make things easy for them. For those of us that weren't born talented and want to become talent, we can. You just must be committed to it.

The commitment isn't to the thing you're doing or the people you're doing it with. The commitment is to yourself to be the best version of you that you need to be to complete the task at hand. Like parenting for instance. It's easy to become a parent; you just got to have sex. But being a good parent that is prepared and financially stable and mature enough to handle having someone's life in their hands is far more superior than someone just having a baby.

I made this mistake. I got married in Las Vegas after knowing someone only 6 months and had two kids with her in under two years' time. I had my kids too early because I was living too fast. I wasn't mature enough or mentally stable enough to raise children, and because of this, my kids have had to pay for my immaturity in their lives and I'm humiliated for it. This will haunt me till the day I die. I wish I could change things, but I can't. What's done is done, and it's my fault. This is why I don't want you or anyone to make my same mistakes and ruin more lives.

Your childhood should be filled with happiness. Your family should want to see you grow up and prosper. You should want to wake up every day to succeed because you are enough of a reason. But all this comes with time and wisdom. No one is ready to be a parent at a young age because how can you teach someone anything when you yourself are too young to know anything? You might know your world, but at that age, you know nothing about the world.

Be young and learn about the world. Come to your own conclusions and explore the planet in your youth. You only get today once. Tomorrow is missed time. Learn as much as you can because life may be what you make it, but knowledge is the key to success. With knowledge, you can unlock any door that is holding you back. Live out your youth because you only get it once.

Don't be like me and millions of others that choose to struggle but never knew it was our own fault. Our childhood and younger years were spent acting like we were older, and we never got to feel what it's like to live in the moment and enjoy the life we were given because we were too busy playing a part in the world we were fictionally making.

Maybe if we stopped saying things like "stop acting so childish," people wouldn't think childish is a bad thing. Being a child is the point in our lives where we learn. We absorb the things we see in the world around us, and that becomes our understanding of the world. It is a simple and innocent time in our lives that is the most important time for development, and it should be treated as the best time of our lives and not be demonized.

I grew up too fast because I wanted to be something I wasn't, which ended up making me someone I wasn't. I lost who I was. I lost opportunities that are irreplaceable, and it was all because I chose to be something I wasn't. If you slow down and enjoy your life, I promise that you will have a better understanding of the real person you are. My mistakes have happened and cannot be reversed; they can only be repaired. But those scars will forever be in my mind. I regret losing my kids daily. Don't be like me and hate the things you've done. You're still young, slow down, and pace yourself.

Set Boundaries for Yourself and Others
Chapter Six

Have you ever heard the phrase "Go with the flow, and see where life takes you"? It sounds like a fun concept, the idea that fate will guide you to your destiny. However, most successful people figured out their life plan early, laying the foundation for their future success. Many people I knew who didn't have a life plan and ended up winging it learned many hard lessons, just like I did.

Boundaries are important in understanding who you are. They help you understand your likes and dislikes. Personal boundaries create the limitations and circumstances you are willing to endure or avoid. We must not only set boundaries for others in our lives but also boundaries for ourselves. These boundaries should be a significant part of your life plan. You need to know when you've had enough of something. These limitations and boundaries also help you understand when you need to take action when life falls off course.

Think about the world around you. Everything has rules. Schools have rules, jobs have rules, our society has rules known as laws. If you want to do just about anything in this world, you must learn the rules first. Rules are the boundaries within a formula for making things go the right way or the wrong way. If you bake cookies, you have to know the right recipe, so your cookies come out perfect and delicious. You can't just throw the ingredients onto a cookie sheet and expect cookies to be the outcome. You have to mix the ingredients together and cook them at the right temperature; otherwise, you end up making a big mess and wasting your time.

If you notice that everything has rules, regulations, and parameters in the world around you, then it is time to realize that's because following the rules is the best way to accomplish something the right way. So, if everything has rules, shouldn't your life? It turns out life is a lot like making cookies. You can either follow the recipe and do it the right way, or it will end up being a big mess and wasted time.

I never made a life plan; I winged it. Without a life plan, I never set boundaries for myself and others because I didn't know what direction my life was going in. When you're young and living life by the seat of your pants, you might not think boundaries are important—I know I didn't. Once I started drinking and doing drugs, I went all out. Why not try everything? I didn't have boundaries or limits. Remember, I was only 10 years old the first time I blacked out from alcohol.

In all, I have overdosed a total of 19 times, with medical records to prove it. The worst was taking so many different pills I fell into a coma. These temporary escapes had lasting consequences. I seriously shouldn't be alive. I have clinically died and been revived a few different times. I have suffered brain damage and taken years off my life because I wanted to see where life would take me. I have been arrested for being so intoxicated that I became incoherent and violent. I never just had a little fun; I had to go full force.

Because of this, I had to spend time in jail, lots of time apologizing for my actions, and even lost a lot of people in my life. Drugs and alcohol became my best friends, and I did whatever they told me to. I thought this behavior was normal, and people should forgive me, and I was angry when they held me accountable for my actions. I was a mess. My life was tanking, but the money in my pocket had my brain convinced otherwise. I was going down fast and taking everyone with me.

I allowed other people's lives to control mine. I spent more time helping my friends and family than I ever spent on bettering myself. These mistakes later turned me to infidelity and other deep-rooted issues I have had to deal with and apologize for, all because I didn't set boundaries. I have made mistakes time and time again because I was always looking for a way out of the life I was living. I could see no future for myself because I didn't know who I was. I never stopped and thought, "How can I change?" I just expected something to magically happen for me.

I needed a life plan. I was always good at figuring out loopholes to rules throughout my life. In my personal life, I did the same thing; I made loopholes for my brain to accept my bad decisions and behaviors. I was convincing myself that those things could wait. Like school, friendships, or work. I never thought of others and their feelings. I only cared about myself. But without a life plan to follow, I just tried to figure it out, and that made things ten times as hard.

I had no one trying to help me understand how important a life plan was. I just heard "you need to change," but I didn't know how. I lied to myself and said this will turn out okay. But I was just letting time pass by that I would never get to replace. I still live with my own demons and have my own personal struggles that I have to face every day. But now that I have set boundaries in my life, I now know my path and why I'm doing what I do, and who it is for. It's for me.

The thing about life is that you get to choose what you want to do with your life. You can wing it like I did and see how messy things get. Or you can listen to my message and realize that your power is in making decisions, decisions that will help you mold the outcome of your life. You can mold it the right way and reap the benefits, or you can see if something will just magically fall into place. I know from my experience that when you don't have a life plan, you just follow what others are doing and end up losing sight of who you are.

Instead of having a plan and being able to write a different story, I chose to see where life took me. I had no rules for myself, no limitations, and no one was going to tell me anything. I thought I had it all figured out. My reality ended up being something that took years to be proud of. I was a late bloomer because I had no clue what I was doing or who I was. This story can end up being your story if you don't start thinking about your future now.

You can either have a big house on top of a hill, drive a fancy car, be successful, live a great and amazing life, or you could be like me and barely have something to show for the years of your life on this planet. It's embarrassing to have to see people from my past and explain why my life turned out the way it did. I will have to live with these regrets I have because I winged it and learned the hard way that life is tough, and all I was doing was making it tougher.

What I wish I knew back then was that I oversaw my own destiny. Every minute of time I could have spent learning who I was and becoming the best version of me I could be was spent on other people or being high. Not having boundaries allowed me to commit bad behaviors like lying, infidelity, and other immoral acts that hurt the people I loved and cared about. I didn't know how to stop myself because I didn't have boundaries. I was too busy thinking an apology could fix things.

I hate looking in the mirror on some days because I hate seeing the person responsible for how my life turned out. The shame I bear is hard to face, but I have to do it to get to where I want to be. It's in the past, and the past is done.

Today, I take my therapy sessions seriously and promote getting mentally healthy. I have changed and keep working on myself daily. Right now, you can choose the life you want and have always dreamed of, or you can wing it. The thing about wanting something is that it's always better when you accomplish it on your own. Pat yourself on the back from time to time because you are enough of a reason to set boundaries. You can set personal, mental, emotional, and sexual boundaries and limitations so you can better determine what your likes or dislikes are, all while being in close proximity to your life plan and your road to success.

I made so many bad decisions from not having boundaries or limitations. One time a buddy of a buddy talked me into going to the store with him one night at a party. We were pulled over not more than a half-mile away from where we had just left. I had no idea we were in a stolen car, and that the driver had a gun and meth in the car. I was on probation and spent the next three months incarcerated, hating every minute of it. One minute I was at a party having a good time, the next I was in jail. I had made many bad choices like this because I didn't know how to say "No." Your boundaries can keep you moving forward on your road to success, as long as you don't stop focusing on your life plan.

Think before you speak

Chapter Seven

I think we have all heard this before, right? But how often do you bite your tongue? I know I had a big problem with lashing out and saying things out of emotion when I was younger. It wasn't until recently that I changed these ways. Many times, in my life, my excessive use of profanity and vulgarities just simply made me look dumb. That's because your words matter just as much as your behavior matters.

Humans are sensitive creatures. Our emotions can get the best of us from time to time, and we go on the defense. I have said so many things that I regret and wish I could take back. An apology can never fully fix damage inflicted by hurtful words. The thing about the phrase "Think before you speak" is that if you understand the meaning, you can control your emotions in almost any situation. This is an opportunity for you to either prove to yourself that you can be enough of a reason to think before you speak.

We have seen famous and rich people being canceled over things they may have said years or even decades ago. Now we are seeing a transition to a world and society that holds you accountable for your words. I grew up in a different time and was part of the last generation that overused the expression "freedom of speech" when they would say something derogatory or offensive to or about anyone. We grew up seeing racism on television and in Hollywood movies. Most comedy elaborated on racial stereotypes and ethnic differences. So, we said what we thought and apologized later if we felt it was necessary.

Poking fun at one another was how we grew up. If you were born different, you were made fun of for it. We were wrong. We hurt one another to protect ourselves from being hurt by others. This also followed us into our lives as we grew up. Time changes everything, and times were changing. The generations after us were raised in a world far different from ours because education professionals realized we had been doing it all wrong.

Now that I'm older, it sucks to think back on certain things about my childhood that could have been changed if I grew up in a world that was compassionate and helped one another, rather than ridicule each other for our shortcomings. I have always had to deal with a learning disability. I was diagnosed with attention deficit disorder, dyslexia, and dyscalculia which made it hard to answer questions aloud when I was in my elementary school. Instead of growing up in a world where we encourage each other as a substitute for insulting each other, maybe I wouldn't have gotten into so many fights. Who knows?

By me not addressing my learning disability and understanding how to overcome it, I grew up angry at the world for making me different and one of the dumb kids in school. I was never dumb or stupid; I was mentally lazy and too busy wanting to fit in to focus on myself to better my future. All this bottled up inside me. As I got older, I would speak in an ignorant tone with a thug twang to my enunciations that made me sound uneducated. I was playing the part.

What I didn't know was that my inability to grow up was because I hadn't dealt with all my pent-up anger that would cause me to lash out and attack my opposition. I was not stupid, but I was acting stupid and dumb. My mouth got me in a lot of trouble. I didn't think before I spoke; I just retaliated.

I was raised in a family of fighters. All of us have this same toxic problem. I can say my family has never fixed a single problem by uniting and having a family meeting. We have all just fought one another from as far back as I can remember. We fought till exhaustion. That's how you won, by exhausting your opponents out.

When I entered the real world, this was how I behaved. I was obnoxious and outright immature. I would not care who was around; I was going to be me and say what I wanted. But everything I was saying had no value. My words proved my mental immaturity, and I was the only one unaware of it. My upbringing prepared me to be vicious and malicious as I got older. I knew how to hurt someone with words that would make them hate themselves. A talent I'm utterly ashamed of.

I used this talent repeatedly in my life, digging a deeper hole of apologies to get out of. The thing about being angry is that you end up only hurting yourself. The way you react matters and the words you use matter. I was always told I was smart, but I never realized it. I just thought people were being nice because I felt I wasn't smart because I had a learning disability. I hated reading, which left me with a limited vocabulary, and those words were all I knew. I limited myself to learning more because I was too busy trying to fit in.

My words ended up defining me. An F-bomb after every other word was just how I spoke. Never using the term "female, women, or woman." Referring to the elderly as "old fucks," which were words I was telling myself, blocking me from seeing the wisdom and experience behind these individuals and only seeing them as in the way or as an annoyance. Talking to people like they were beneath me when I was the one uneducated. The part I was playing had me talking like an idiot and my brain saw nothing wrong with it because I didn't know better. I thought I was cool.

I was disrespectful to the women and people in my life. Some of them have had to apologize for my words, and I dislike myself for that. What you say can be the difference between someone seeing you as either smart or stupid. Think about that person you know that constantly has to argue for no reason whatsoever. It's annoying, right? The type that embarrasses the people they're with. That was me.

I hate thinking about it and cringe at the thought of who I used to be. What it taught me was that I needed to grow up because no adult in the real world takes anyone seriously that acts and talks like that. I may have had money, but money wasn't the currency I needed. I needed to educate myself to learn how to speak to others to buy my way into society. I was stuck in my world; I didn't even know the real world existed. I thought I knew everything, and the truth was I knew nothing.

The best thing I ever did for myself was learn how to communicate properly with others. I was a full-grown adult and missed out on a lot of opportunities because of learning this late in life. If I knew then that each interaction matters, and that your behavior matters, I would have also known that my words mattered, I would have gotten so much farther in life. I hurt a lot of people's feelings due to things I have said, but what ultimately happened was me hurting myself. My reputation was tarnished, and I lived a life of losses. I lost a family, friends, and my children because I didn't realize how powerful my words were.

"I'm sorry" never fully fixes things. I now live a better life, but my past is full of regrets I brought on myself. Thinking before you speak can be the difference between you living an amazing life full of friends and family, or a life of misery and remorse; the choice is yours. People are absolutely going to judge you for the things you say, and what you say will play a huge role in how that person sees you in their perception.

Realize that you can be kind, caring, and courteous; it's okay. Not everything has to be sarcastic or made fun of. Your words are important, and they mold people's impressions of you. I thought I was cool for being a rebel; truth is, I was just an uneducated jackass looking for acceptance. If I had just accepted myself for who I was at a young age, I probably wouldn't have ended up living the life I led and saying the things I said. I would have done better, and all it would have taken was me just thinking before speaking.

Next time you're upset, stop and think about your words. Don't just react. Take a breath and think about what you want as an outcome. Don't just win the fight. It's not worth it. Your emotions are going to get the best of you from time to time; that's just life. Controlling your words is a powerful skill that can make you stand out in a world of fighters. Be rational when you speak and think about how you want to be heard. You can sound like a genius or a jackass; that choice is yours.

If I had thought about my words and their message, I could have saved myself a lot of embarrassment and self-loathing. A lot of my life turned out the way it did because I didn't think before speaking. If I would have, I probably wouldn't have lied so much, been so disrespectful, or hidden from myself for so long. I was so wrong, but I didn't learn from my mistake until some of my relationships were too lost and broken to repair. Don't be like me. Be smarter and think before you speak.

Learn Tolerance

Chapter 8

Have you ever pondered over all the time you've squandered? From counting sheep, standing in line, or sitting in waiting rooms. We all detest wasting our time on something we consider unworthy of it. The truth is most of our time isn't wasted on these moments or situations. Instead, it's often spent on the people we choose to keep closest in our lives.

We all harbor a certain set of expectations within ourselves regarding how others should act and treat us. Unfortunately, this self-imposed expectation often leads to pain and turmoil. Assuming that others prioritize our intentions over their own, or that someone else will bring us happiness and contentment, is a fallacy we're all guilty of. We tend to forget that we receive what we give. In other words, if we want people to treat us right, we must treat them with the same dignity. Ah, the old golden rule most of us learned in kindergarten resurfaces as the key to unlocking what makes people either love or hate us.

We all desire to be loved and respected, and we often disapprove of those who don't align with our own ideals. Here's where tolerance comes into play! Tolerance is an incredible gift we can give to our brain, heart, and soul. You see, we've been misled all our lives, being told that we are all equal. Conceptually, we are indeed equal in terms of our civil liberties and the opportunities that reinforce our human and governmental rights. However, we are all vastly different. We are products of our environments and heritage. A tall person is not the same as a short person, just as a slender person isn't the same as someone fuller and more robust. Each person grapples with their own genetics, emotions, mental stability, and physical appearance. These struggles shape the unique realities we each inhabit. What we lack in one area often gets compensated for in other aspects of our lives, giving rise to personality traits and characteristics that form our identities.

As we grow and mature, these self-perceptions become our reality, shaping the world and universe our minds reside in. We become less considerate of others and assume that "they should be just like me." We expect people to think and react as we do, fantasizing about what we would do in their shoes, without fully understanding their situation, circumstances, or backstory. We play the role of gurus and walking encyclopedias, thinking we have endless knowledge.

In a world teeming with experts and know-it-alls, we tend to find comfort within our social circles, where we feel accepted and at ease. Sociology terms this our social group; our primary social group is often our family or guardians who raised us. As we discover our own preferences and dislikes, we gravitate towards people who share similar interests, creating common ground for discussions and interactions. As children, we bond with others who enjoy the same sports and games or share literary interests. Much of this knowledge is instilled in us during childhood and youth by our social groups and economic circumstances.

A wealthy child may experience different places through family travels, while a less financially stable family might travel less during the child's adolescence, as was my case. Each experience becomes a memory etched in our minds. When someone disappoints us or hurts our feelings, we tend to heal by establishing barriers and walls to protect ourselves from pain. Just as a physical wound transforms from a fresh injury to a scab, then a scar serving as a reminder of our past hurts, our ego, pride, and self-image can scar our minds, affecting our self-esteem. So, we seek out people, pets, and things that make us feel happy, better, and safe, hoping they will fill the voids and emotional potholes along life's journey.

If we reflect far enough, we can all recall a moment that profoundly impacted us, altering our perspective on life. It might have been a humiliating public embarrassment by a friend, sibling, or parent, or something more traumatic like the loss of a loved one. Regardless, these experiences shape who we are and craft our life stories.

Unfortunately, we aren't taught much about tolerating ourselves or the environments we grew up in. Instead, we are told to love ourselves without being given the tools on how to do so. Thus, when someone or something comes along and shows us love, we attach ourselves to them, filling emotional voids and potholes created by life's challenges.

We become emotionally devoted to these individuals, giving them the love we yearn for in return. We may adjust our behaviors, communication styles, or even life habits to make them happier, sacrificing our own preferences in the process.

That's a lot of power! In fact, this power often leads to heartbreak and sorrow. This is where and when we need to arm ourselves with a powerful weapon that can protect our emotions—tolerance! It may sound unusual, but bear with me.

The feeling of love can be intoxicating, and if the love itself is toxic, it may take time to realize the love hangover that leaves us spinning and ready to vomit is not genuine love at all. Many of us mistake falling for someone with falling in love with them, but these are distinct experiences. Love entails significant commitment and responsibility, concepts that many of us misunderstand.

We may think that living together, marriage, and shared bank accounts symbolize love because that's what we've been taught. Loyalty becomes a word tied to our own needs rather than its true definition. Loyalty should mean, "no matter what happens, I'm here for you." Dogs exemplify loyalty in their unwavering devotion. They correct a pack member's misbehavior but remain fiercely protective when faced with external threats, showcasing true loyalty.

I'm not advocating for violence or endorsing physical attacks within social groups. However, it's fascinating how wild animals often grasp concepts like loyalty better than supposedly civilized species.

My interpretation of loyalty has garnered me some puzzled looks in life. I believe that loyalty is primal and selfless—a two-way street. If you expect loyalty from others but cannot accept that they're imperfect humans capable of mistakes that may hurt you, then you don't grasp the true meaning of loyalty. Human beings make mistakes, and loyalty means working through those mistakes together, facing discomfort and pain while communicating openly.

This is where tolerance becomes crucial for effective communication. We must learn to tolerate our feelings rather than react impulsively. From birth, the only thing truly ours is our feelings. Understanding this earlier in life would have been invaluable. We choose whether to be in control or out of control of our emotions, influencing our decisions and actions. Our feelings guide us in everything, from our food choices to how we cancel plans last minute, often without considering how our actions impact others.

Tolerance is the ability or willingness to accept opinions or behaviors that differ from our own. It's about being patient, understanding, and accepting of differences. Tolerance builds resilience, fortitude, and empathy, enabling us to appreciate beliefs or practices that may conflict with our own. But what about tolerating ourselves?

It starts with honesty. Earlier in this chapter, we discussed wasting time on people who may not deserve it, often because we tolerate everyone else before tolerating ourselves. This negative form of tolerance can introduce toxic elements into our lives.

Tolerance fosters less stress and greater happiness in our communities. It means acknowledging that differences have a right to exist, whether or not we agree with them. However, accepting something doesn't mean it needs to be a part of our lives. Practicing tolerance removes self-imposed barriers, allowing us to think more broadly and find inner peace. This power enables us to discern what we will or will not allow in our lives.

By respecting ourselves and appreciating our own existence, we can truly tolerate ourselves. This marks the beginning of self-love.

Self-love is not just about affirmations or superficial acts of kindness toward us. It's about embracing our flaws, acknowledging our strengths, and understanding that we are worthy of love and respect, both from ourselves and others. Tolerance toward ourselves allows us to navigate life's challenges with grace and compassion, fostering a deeper sense of fulfillment and contentment.

In conclusion, learning tolerance is not just about accepting others; it's also about accepting ourselves. When we practice tolerance, we open doors to understanding, empathy, and genuine connection, both within ourselves and with the world around us.

Chapter Nine

Better Yourself

In the journey of life, there comes a time when we realize that the most significant changes start from within. It's not about fixing others or changing external circumstances; it's about bettering ourselves. This chapter delves into the transformative power of self-improvement and personal growth.

One of the pillars of bettering yourself is embracing continuous learning. Life is a never-ending journey of growth, and each experience, whether positive or negative, holds valuable lessons. By staying curious, open-minded, and willing to learn from every situation, you enrich your understanding of the world and yourself.

Central to bettering yourself is cultivating self-love and acceptance. Acknowledge your strengths, but also embrace your flaws and imperfections. It's through self-compassion that you pave the way for genuine growth. Treat yourself with kindness, forgive your mistakes, and celebrate your achievements, no matter how small they may seem.

Setting meaningful goals gives direction and purpose to your journey of self-improvement. Define what success means to you, both personally and professionally. Break down larger goals into manageable steps and stay committed to taking consistent actions towards achieving them. Remember, progress, not perfection, is the key.

Mindfulness and self-awareness are powerful tools in the quest for personal growth. Cultivate mindfulness by being present in the moment, observing your thoughts and emotions without judgment. Self-awareness involves knowing your strengths, weaknesses, values, and motivations. It allows you to make conscious choices aligned with your authentic self.

Change is inevitable and embracing it with an open mind is essential for personal evolution. Be adaptable and resilient in the face of challenges and setbacks. View change as an opportunity for growth and transformation rather than a threat. Embracing change fosters agility and empowers you to navigate life's twists and turns with grace.

Surround yourself with positive influences and foster healthy relationships. Build a support network of friends, mentors, and loved ones who uplift and inspire you. Healthy relationships provide encouragement, constructive feedback, and a sense of belonging, contributing to your overall well-being and personal development.

Self-care is not selfish; it's a crucial aspect of self-improvement. Prioritize your physical, mental, and emotional well-being by engaging in activities that nourish your body, mind, and soul. This includes regular exercise, healthy eating, adequate rest, mindfulness practices, hobbies you enjoy, and seeking support when needed.

Regularly reflect on your progress, evaluate your goals and priorities, and be willing to adjust course if necessary. Self-improvement is a dynamic process that requires self-reflection, honesty, and a willingness to adapt. Celebrate your successes, learn from your challenges, and use feedback to refine your path forward.

Bettering yourself is an ongoing journey fueled by self-love, continuous learning, goal setting, mindfulness, adaptability, healthy relationships, self-care, and self-reflection. Embrace this journey wholeheartedly, for it leads to personal fulfillment, growth, and a meaningful life aligned with your values and aspirations. Remember, the power to better yourself lies within you.

Conclusion

Embracing Life's Journey

As we reach the conclusion of this book, it's essential to reflect on the profound insights and transformative journey we've explored together. "Emancipate yourselves from mental slavery, none but ourselves can free our minds." These powerful words from Bob Marley's 'Redemption Song' resonate deeply, reminding us of the liberation found in self-awareness, growth, and self-love.

Throughout these pages, we've delved into the complexities of my life, acknowledging that it's okay to make mistakes and stumble along the way. "Every little thing is gonna be alright," setbacks and challenges are opportunities for growth and learning. It's through embracing our imperfections and learning from our experiences that we truly evolve and become stronger.

Self-love is not selfish; it's a foundational pillar that allows us to navigate life's twists and turns with resilience, compassion, and authenticity. Embrace each day with gratitude, courage, and an open heart, knowing that every experience, triumph, and challenge contributes to the beautiful tapestry of your life's story.

I encourage you to:

1. Embrace self-love and acceptance, celebrating your uniqueness and embracing your journey.
2. Cultivate a growth mindset, viewing challenges as opportunities for learning and growth.
3. Foster healthy relationships built on trust, respect, and mutual support.
4. Practice self-care and prioritize your well-being, nurturing your body, mind, and soul.
5. Set meaningful goals aligned with your values and aspirations and take consistent steps towards achieving them.
6. Embrace change and adaptability, recognizing that life's journey is dynamic and ever evolving.

Thank you for embarking on this journey with me. Here's to embracing life's journey and becoming the best version of ourselves, one step at a time.